Orion,

My Son, I Love You...

Forever, for Always, and No Matter What!

Love you and am so proud of you

Mom

ISBN: 978-1-59842-869-8

Wonderful Wacky Women®

Inspiring•Uplifting•Empowering

is a trademark of Suzy and Al Toronto. Used under license.

Ħ and Blue Mountain Press are registered in U.S. Patent and Trademark Office. Certain trademarks are used under license.

Printed in China.
Fourth Printing: 2018

⊕ This book is printed on recycled paper.

This book is printed on paper that has been specially produced to be acid free (neutral pH) and contains no groundwood or unbleached pulp. It conforms with the requirements of the American National Standards Institute, Inc., so as to ensure that this book will last and be enjoyed by future generations.

Blue Mountain Arts, Inc.

P.O. Box 4549, Boulder, Colorado 80306

My Son, I Love You...

Forever, for Always, and No Matter What!

Suzy Toronto

Blue Mountain Press™
Boulder, Colorado

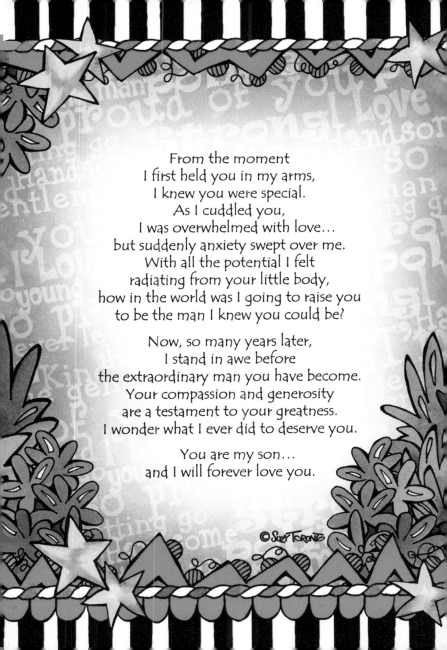

From the moment
I first held you in my arms,
I knew you were special.
As I cuddled you,
I was overwhelmed with love…
but suddenly anxiety swept over me.
With all the potential I felt
radiating from your little body,
how in the world was I going to raise you
to be the man I knew you could be?

Now, so many years later,
I stand in awe before
the extraordinary man you have become.
Your compassion and generosity
are a testament to your greatness.
I wonder what I ever did to deserve you.

You are my son…
and I will forever love you.

©Suzy Toronto

You're More Than My Son...
You're Also My Friend

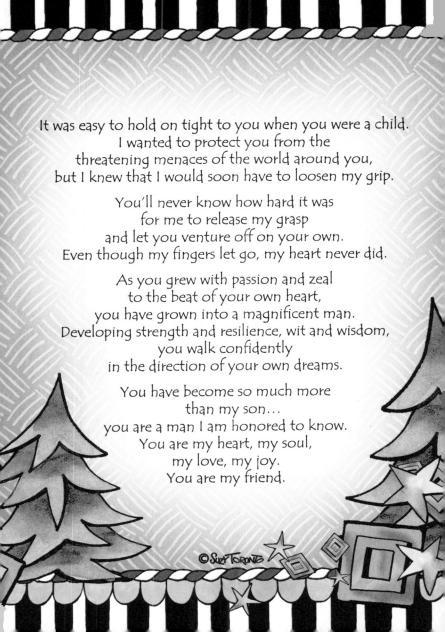

It was easy to hold on tight to you when you were a child.
I wanted to protect you from the
threatening menaces of the world around you,
but I knew that I would soon have to loosen my grip.

You'll never know how hard it was
for me to release my grasp
and let you venture off on your own.
Even though my fingers let go, my heart never did.

As you grew with passion and zeal
to the beat of your own heart,
you have grown into a magnificent man.
Developing strength and resilience, wit and wisdom,
you walk confidently
in the direction of your own dreams.

You have become so much more
than my son…
you are a man I am honored to know.
You are my heart, my soul,
my love, my joy.
You are my friend.

© Suzy Toronto

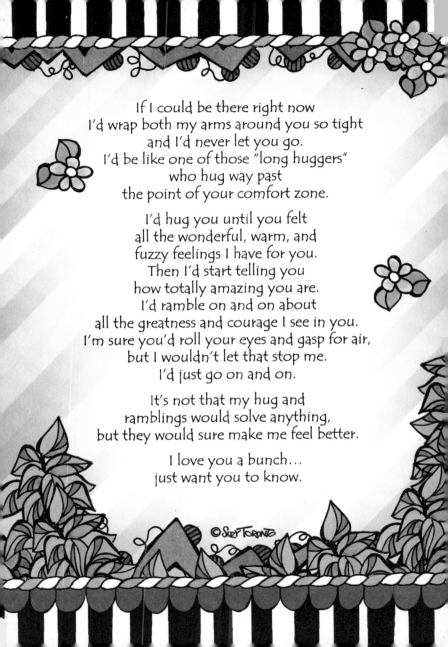

If I could be there right now
I'd wrap both my arms around you so tight
and I'd never let you go.
I'd be like one of those "long huggers"
who hug way past
the point of your comfort zone.

I'd hug you until you felt
all the wonderful, warm, and
fuzzy feelings I have for you.
Then I'd start telling you
how totally amazing you are.
I'd ramble on and on about
all the greatness and courage I see in you.
I'm sure you'd roll your eyes and gasp for air,
but I wouldn't let that stop me.
I'd just go on and on.

It's not that my hug and
ramblings would solve anything,
but they would sure make me feel better.

I love you a bunch...
just want you to know.

© Suzy Toronto

Wonderful Wacky Words...
Wisdom for My Son

Think big... if that doesn't work, think bigger.

It's okay to build yourself a man cave, but use it sparingly.

Life is all about how you handle Plan B — in the end it will be the truest test of your character.

Be nice. Play fair. Forgive everyone.

Nothing is as strong as a man who can be tender — or as weak as a man who thinks he has to be tough.

It's okay to ask for directions.

When you are faced with disappointment, get over it, be done with it, and get on with it.

You were born to shine — let your inner light illuminate the world.

Always be a hug waiting to happen.

If you want rainbows, you gotta have rain.

When life gives you a second chance, take it.

Stop what you're doing and start living every minute of your life to the fullest.

Rise by lifting others up. Expect miracles.

Always remember and never forget: you are loved.

When you were little, you followed me around,
watched every move I made,
and tried to be just like me.
No matter what I did, you were my little shadow.

I never quite felt worthy of the honor,
but it made me smile all over.
I guess it's one of the rights of parenthood,
and I loved every minute of it.

But now, as I see the incredible man you have become,
it's clear how great you turned out in spite of my example!
It's not supposed to happen that way.
There definitely was an unseen hand in your life,
for which I will always be grateful.

You have grown into an amazing person,
exceeded all my expectations,
and left me in the dust.

Now the tables have turned…
and I wish I could be just like you.

©Suzy Toronto

You Are the World's
Greatest Son

I know how much you love long, sappy speeches that drone on and on about what a wonderful son you are. And I know you especially like it when I describe how amazing, brilliant, fabulous, and really terrific I think you are. If I had my way, I'd write a full-length novel just to make sure it covered all the important stuff... filled with every possible adjective I could think of... like magnificent, stupendous, astounding, fantastic, marvelous... Well, you get the idea! Are you rolling your eyes yet? Okay, okay: I admit I've been known to gush a bit too much. So in order to spare you any further endurance tests, I've prepared this short, yet heartfelt message for you...

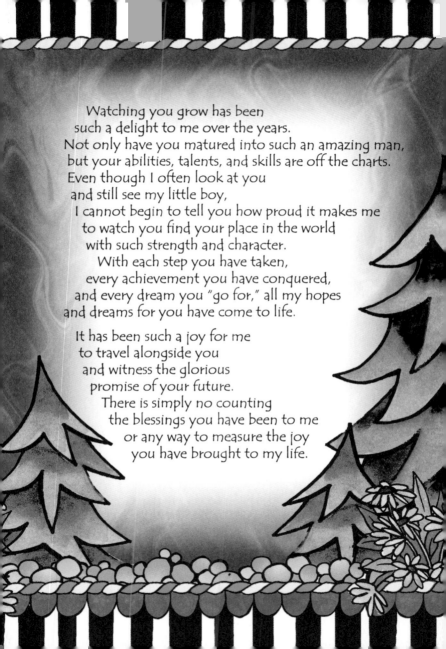

Watching you grow has been
such a delight to me over the years.
Not only have you matured into such an amazing man,
but your abilities, talents, and skills are off the charts.
Even though I often look at you
and still see my little boy,
I cannot begin to tell you how proud it makes me
to watch you find your place in the world
with such strength and character.
With each step you have taken,
every achievement you have conquered,
and every dream you "go for," all my hopes
and dreams for you have come to life.

It has been such a joy for me
to travel alongside you
and witness the glorious
promise of your future.
There is simply no counting
the blessings you have been to me
or any way to measure the joy
you have brought to my life.

How to Live a Life Worth Loving

Just Stop, Listen, and Learn

Stop. Stop churning through those endless, pointless cycles that blind you from appreciating that the world around you is so much bigger than your immediate crisis. Stop focusing inward, and look beyond yourself. Stop ignoring the rich opportunities for growth that you've passed up, simply because you were afraid. Stop hauling around your unnecessary baggage — whether it's emotional or physical. Unburden yourself from the constant repetition of reliving each mistake or wrong done to you. None of it serves to inspire, uplift, or empower another human being... least of all you!

Listen. Listen to your breathing, to your heartbeat. Listen to the sound of the ocean, the rustle of leaves in the wind, and the silence of softly falling snow. Stop talking… and really take the time to just listen. Seek out those who have accomplished astonishing feats, and listen to what they have to say. Absorb all that is good in them, and let the rest drift away. Drink in the wisdom they have to offer. Such wisdom is everywhere, if you will just open your heart and listen…

© Suzy Toronto

Learn. Learn from your parents. Learn from your children. Learn from those who love you — and, even more, from those who don't. Admit that you are not always right and that you don't have all the answers. Try to look at every situation from another perspective. Learn to take a chance and make a change. Accept obstacles and challenges as opportunities to grow and become a better person. These are among our greatest gifts, but we must have the grace to accept them.

© Suzy Toronto

Here's the real irony of life:
  in order for growth to be all about you,
    you have to stop thinking about yourself,
      listen to the wisdom of those around you,
      and learn from it all.

   See?
    It's easy.

Just stop, listen, and learn.

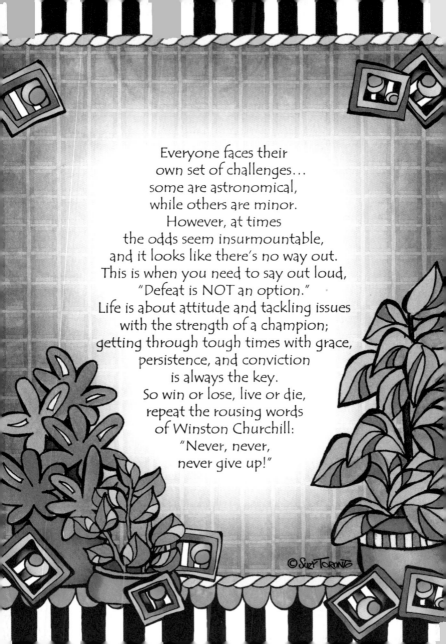

Everyone faces their
own set of challenges...
some are astronomical,
while others are minor.
However, at times
the odds seem insurmountable,
and it looks like there's no way out.
This is when you need to say out loud,
"Defeat is NOT an option."
Life is about attitude and tackling issues
with the strength of a champion;
getting through tough times with grace,
persistence, and conviction
is always the key.
So win or lose, live or die,
repeat the rousing words
of Winston Churchill:
"Never, never,
never give up!"

©Suzy Toronto

Make 5,372 Epic Mistakes on Purpose!

People mess up a lot.
And I'm not talking about little,
unnoticeable flubs.
I'm talking all-out spectacles to behold…
epic stuff that legends are made of.
But here is the secret that few people know —
you should make a lot of mistakes on purpose.
That's right!
Whenever you start something new,
have a goal to make as many mistakes
as rapidly as you can,
so you can learn
as much as possible
in the shortest period of time —
even if you have to make
5,372 mistakes for it to sink in.

Never, ever be ashamed to find the error of
your ways or the faults in your understanding.
Mistakes, both big and small, are not failures
unless you fail to learn from them.
   They are simply steppingstones to progress,
   knowledge, and success.
      So try to do everything you can to learn
         as much as possible from your mistakes...
            as well as those of others too.

            This is where I come in. I'm here to help.
         There are simply not enough hours in the day
      to make all the mistakes yourself.
Together we can double the effort,
   double the results,
      and double the fun —
         plus, I bet we'll make a real crack team!
         So let's join forces and mess up
            right alongside each other.
               Let's attempt the impossible —
                  even if it takes 5,372
                     mistakes to achieve!

It's OK to Grab a Tiger by the Tail...

Even If You Don't Know What to Do Next!

Sometimes flying by the seat of your pants can get a little crazy — kind of like grabbing a tiger by the tail with no clue what to do next. Most of my life, I have thrown caution to the wind, jumped in with both feet, and learned to swim on the way up.

But things don't always go as planned. Many times the water was too deep or the wings I expected never appeared… sometimes both! But every time I dry myself off and get ready to try again, I don't focus on the misjudged leap or how I must have embarrassed myself beyond belief *that* time. Because the real tragedy would be if I had never even tried.

Reaching outside your comfort zone and taking a chance is worth any bumps and bruises you might get along the way. Once your adventure has begun, you'll find the trip is a kick, the possibilities are endless, and the journey is truly amazing.

So seriously, what are you waiting for? You have the power, knowledge, and drive inside you to perform extraordinary feats, but you have to be willing to risk it… you have to grab that tiger's tail and hang on for dear life as it swings you around.

All progress comes from daring to begin.
So take a deep breath, and enjoy the ride!

© Suzy Toronto

Words of Wisdom for Guys to Live By

Don't do dumb stuff (you know what!).

Reach outside your comfort zone…
it's not as hard as you think.

Don't wait to live your dreams…
jump in with both feet and go for them!

There's no such thing as "can't"…
you CAN do anything.

Life is all about how you handle Plan B.

To stand out in a crowd, be outstanding.

Learn to dream with your eyes wide open.

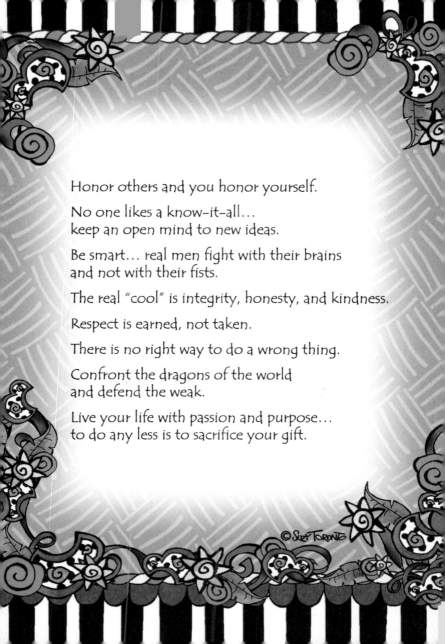

Honor others and you honor yourself.

No one likes a know-it-all...
keep an open mind to new ideas.

Be smart... real men fight with their brains
and not with their fists.

The real "cool" is integrity, honesty, and kindness.

Respect is earned, not taken.

There is no right way to do a wrong thing.

Confront the dragons of the world
and defend the weak.

Live your life with passion and purpose...
to do any less is to sacrifice your gift.

© Suzy Toronto

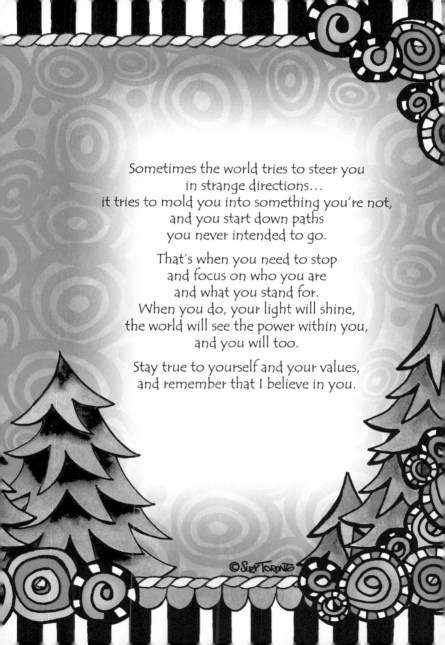

Sometimes the world tries to steer you
in strange directions...
it tries to mold you into something you're not,
and you start down paths
you never intended to go.

That's when you need to stop
and focus on who you are
and what you stand for.
When you do, your light will shine,
the world will see the power within you,
and you will too.

Stay true to yourself and your values,
and remember that I believe in you.

© Suzy Toronto

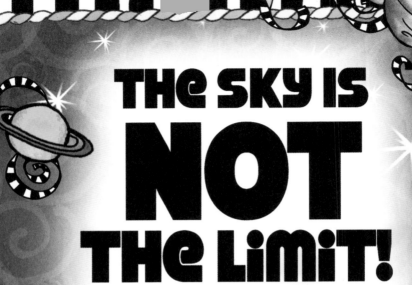

THE SKY IS NOT THE LIMIT!

(I'm pretty sure there are footprints on the moon)

Every time I hear someone exclaim,
"The sky's the limit!" with gusto and exuberance,
my reaction is always the same.
I want to shake them within an inch of their life
and cry, "Oh ye of little faith and withered dreams!"

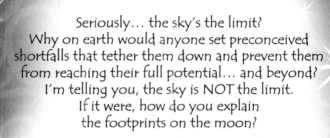

Seriously… the sky's the limit?
Why on earth would anyone set preconceived
shortfalls that tether them down and prevent them
from reaching their full potential… and beyond?
I'm telling you, the sky is NOT the limit.
If it were, how do you explain
the footprints on the moon?

To soar past obstacles in our paths,
the trick is to simply aim high above them.
Look past the midnight skies where
there are no stars to blind us, no meteors to impede us,
and no gravity to slow us down.
Sure, short-term goals are important steppingstones,
but keep your mind open to warp-drive capability.
With a twinkle in your eye, a smile on your lips,
and purpose in your heart, set your sights
on the infinite possibilities in front of you.
Far beyond your wildest dreams,
you really are limitless in every way.

The opportunity is there.
Decide to make it a reality!

© Suzy Toronto

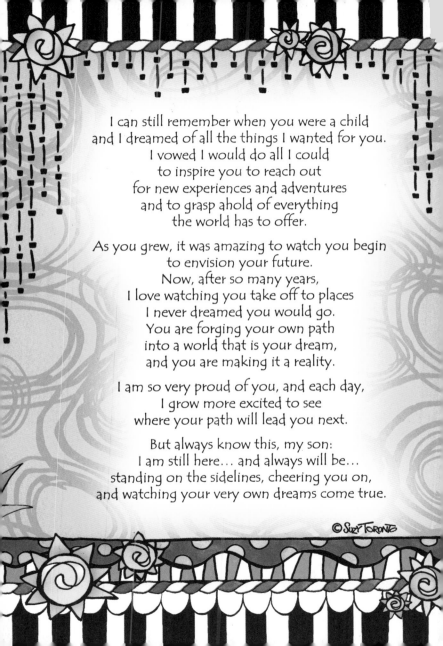

I can still remember when you were a child
and I dreamed of all the things I wanted for you.
I vowed I would do all I could
to inspire you to reach out
for new experiences and adventures
and to grasp ahold of everything
the world has to offer.

As you grew, it was amazing to watch you begin
to envision your future.
Now, after so many years,
I love watching you take off to places
I never dreamed you would go.
You are forging your own path
into a world that is your dream,
and you are making it a reality.

I am so very proud of you, and each day,
I grow more excited to see
where your path will lead you next.

But always know this, my son:
I am still here… and always will be…
standing on the sidelines, cheering you on,
and watching your very own dreams come true.

© Suzy Toronto

When you were a baby, I held you close
and smothered your sweet face with kisses.
I vowed I would never let you go.

When you were a child, I pushed you to study hard
and learn all the good things
from the world around you.

When you were a young man, I encouraged you
to follow your dreams
and be passionate about all your choices.

And then I did the hardest thing I ever had to do...
that which I vowed I would never do:
I let go...

I lied!
I'm never letting go.

© Suzy Toronto

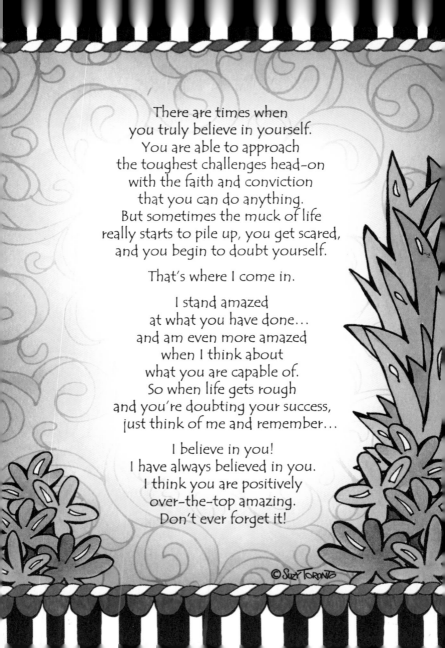

There are times when
you truly believe in yourself.
You are able to approach
the toughest challenges head-on
with the faith and conviction
that you can do anything.
But sometimes the muck of life
really starts to pile up, you get scared,
and you begin to doubt yourself.

That's where I come in.

I stand amazed
at what you have done...
and am even more amazed
when I think about
what you are capable of.
So when life gets rough
and you're doubting your success,
just think of me and remember...

I believe in you!
I have always believed in you.
I think you are positively
over-the-top amazing.
Don't ever forget it!

© Suzy Toronto

About the Author

So this is me… I'm a tad wacky and just shy of crazy. I'm fiftysomething and live in the sleepy village of Tangerine, Florida, with my husband, Al, and a big, goofy dog named Lucy. And because life wasn't crazy enough, my eightysomething-year-old parents live with us too. (In my home, the nuts don't fall far from the tree!) I eat far too much chocolate, and I drink sparkling water by the gallon. I practice yoga, ride a little red scooter, and go to the beach every chance I get. I have five grown children and over a dozen grandkids who love me as much as I adore them. I teach them to dip their French fries in their chocolate shakes and to make up any old words to the tunes they like. But most of all, I teach them to never, ever color inside the lines. This is the Wild Wacky Wonderful life I lead, and I wouldn't have it any other way. Welcome to my world!